W9-BZB-110

SHE
PERSISTED

Published by Sellers Publishing, Inc.

Copyright © 2018 Sellers Publishing, Inc.
Illustrations © 2018 Becca Cahan
All rights reserved.

Sellers Publishing, Inc.
161 John Roberts Road, South Portland, Maine 04106
Visit our website: www.sellerspublishing.com • E-mail: rsp@rsvp.com

Mary L. Baldwin, Managing Editor

Charlotte Cromwell, Production Editor

ISBN 13: 978-1-4162-4666-4

No portion of this book may be reproduced, stored in a retrieval system, or transmitted in any form or by any means, mechanical, electronic, photocopying, recording, or otherwise, without the written permission of the publisher.

10 9 8 7 6 5 4 3 2 1

Printed in China.

SHE PERSISTED

QUOTES to MOTIVATE + INSPIRE

art by
BECCA ♥ CAHAN

SELLERS PUBLISHING

MAYA ANGELOU was an award-winning author, poet, civil rights activist, and recipient of the Presidential Medal of Freedom. She wrote the words, "I'm a woman, phenomenally. Phenomenal woman, that's me."

Her advice to young women of the world: Develop courage.

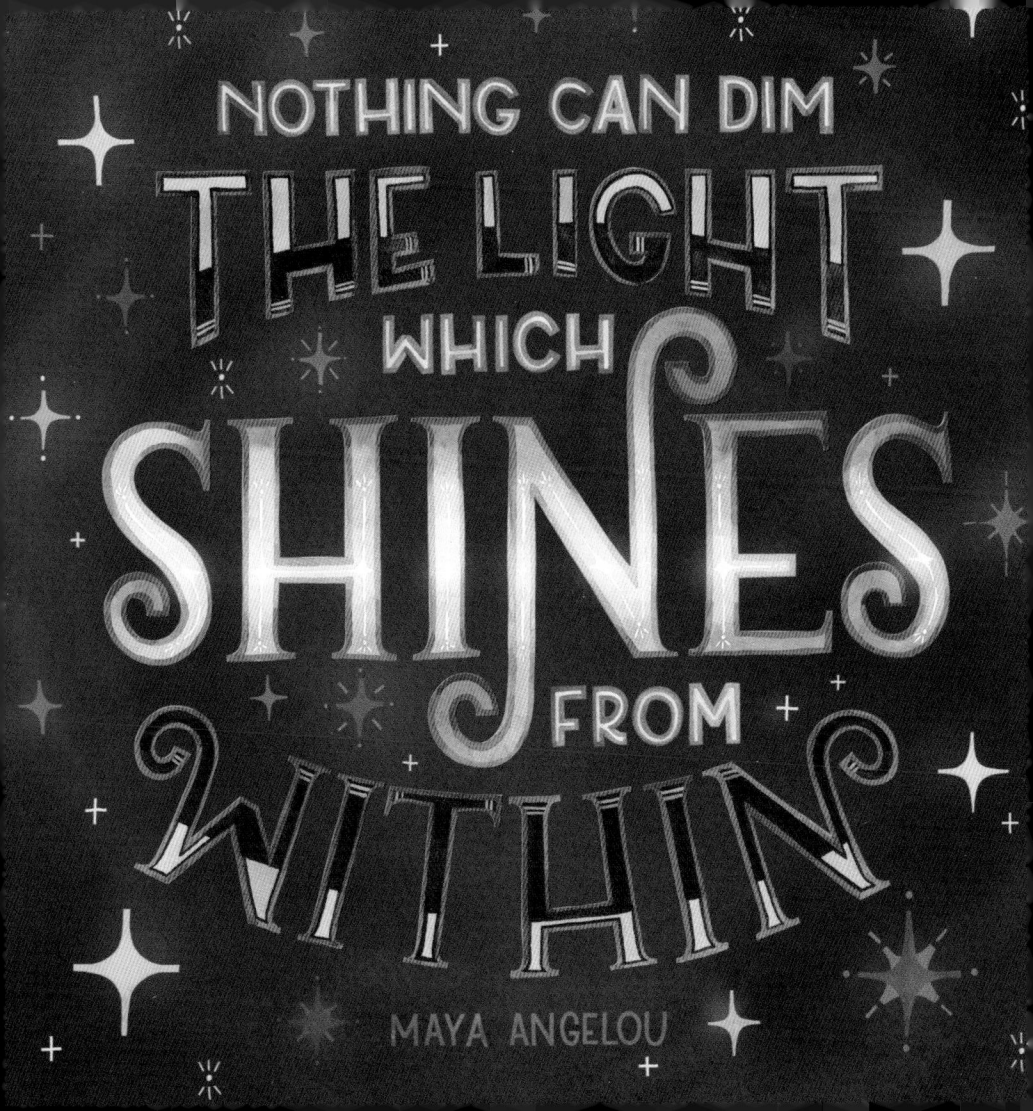
NOTHING CAN DIM
THE LIGHT
WHICH
SHINES
FROM
WITHIN
MAYA ANGELOU

it takes
COURAGE
TO grow UP
& BECOME WHO YOU
really are
e.e. cummings

Bravery:
noun • BRAV·ER·Y \'brav(ə)rē/
courageous behavior
or character

Strength grows in the moments when you think you can't go on but you keep going anyway.

Here's to
STRONG WOMEN.
may we
KNOW THEM.
may we
BE THEM.
may we
RAISE THEM.

There is
NO LIMIT
to what
WE as WOMEN
can
ACCOMPLISH
MICHELLE OBAMA

Former first lady **MICHELLE OBAMA** is a strong advocate for women's rights and believes that a country can never truly flourish if it stifles the potential of its women and deprives itself of the contributions of half of its citizens.

MOMENTUM:

noun • MO·MEN·TUM /mō'men(t)əm/

driving force gained by the
development of a process
or course of events

WHATEVER
YOU DO,
KEEP
MOVING
FORWARD
MARTIN LUTHER KING JR.

WELL-BEHAVED
WOMEN
SELDOM MAKE
HISTORY
LAUREL THATCHER ULRICH

Use your voice.
Use your actions.
MAKE A DIFFERENCE.

As a young girl, MALALA YOUSAFZAI defied the Taliban in Pakistan by demanding that all girls be allowed to receive an education. Against injury and extreme adverstiy, she went on to receive the Nobel Peace Prize in 2014.

i am
STRONGER
than
FEAR
Malala
Yousafzai

SHE IS CLOTHED in
STRENGTH &
DIGNITY
&
SHE LAUGHS
WITHOUT FEAR
of the FUTURE
PROVERBS 31:25

DIGNITY:

noun • DIG·NI·TY /dignədē/
a sense of pride in oneself; self-respect

If you AIM at nothing
you won't hit ANYTHING.

I·AM·SEEKING,
i am
STRIVING
i am in it with
ALL
MY·HEART.
VINCENT·VAN·GOGH

we all have
magic
inside us.
J.K. ROWLING

J.K. Rowling is a British novelist, screenwriter, and producer. In the face of adversity, she went from being a poor, single mother with no job, to writing one of the most popular and successful fantasy series of all times. Rowling credits her imagination, determination, and ability to survive for emerging from her setbacks stronger and wiser.

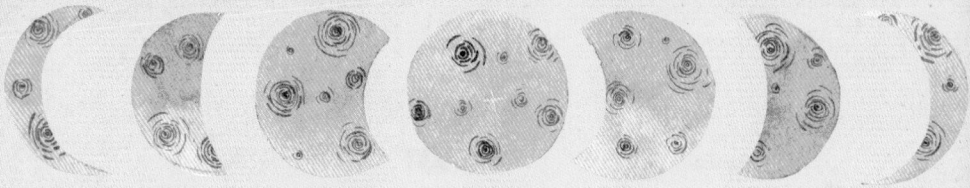

CREATIVITY:

noun • CRE·A·TIV·I·TY /krēā'tivədē

the ability to form new ideas or concepts

IF YOU DON'T
IMAGINE,
NOTHING EVER
HAPPENS
AT ALL.

THE SECRET TO
GETTING AHEAD
IS GETTING
STARTED
AGATHA CHRISTIE

FOLLOW
your
HEART

Eleanor Roosevelt was the longest-serving First Lady throughout her husband's four terms as the 32nd president of the United States. Breaking White House precedence, she gave lectures, held press conferences, and openly expressed her opinions. As an activist for the underprivileged of all races and religions, she played a major role in the drafting and adoption of the Universal Declaration of Human Rights.

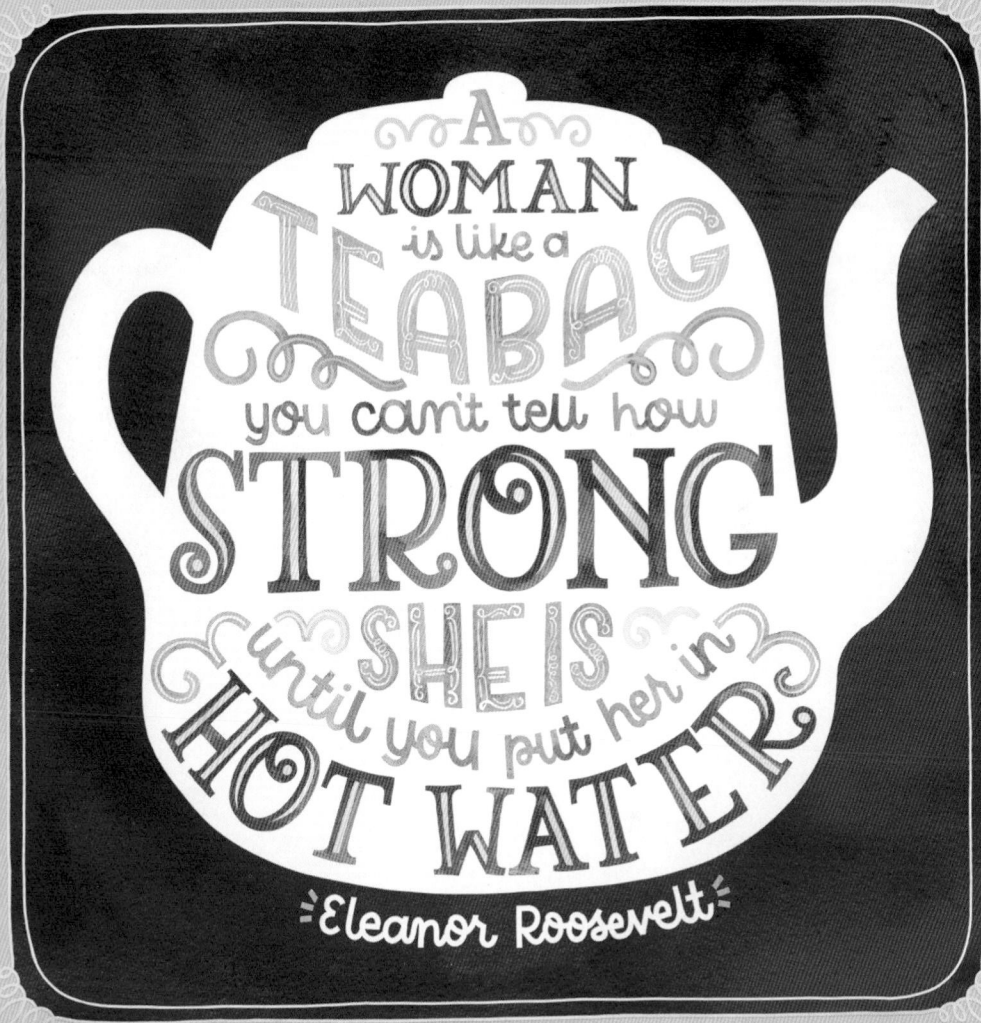
A WOMAN is like a TEABAG you can't tell how STRONG SHE IS until you put her in HOT WATER
Eleanor Roosevelt

Live with
INTENTION
MARY ANN RADMACHER
BECCA CAHAN

Intention:

noun • in·ten·tion \ in'ten(t)SH(ə)n \
purpose, deliberateness, a process, a plan

Life is the greatest challenge there is. Rise up, meet it, and become stronger.

LIFE
is
TOUGH
BUT SO ARE
you

I AM
NOT
AFRAID,
I WAS
BORN TO
DO·THIS
JOAN of ARC

Acting under divine guidance, JOAN OF ARC, a determined 19-year-old peasant girl led the French army to victory over the English. A military leader, and martyr, she was canonized as a saint in 1920.

PERSISTENCE:

noun • PER·SIST·ENCE \pər'sistəns/

steadfast; firm course of action despite opposition

WE MAY ENCOUNTER
MANY
DEFEATS,
BUT WE
MAY NOT
BE
DEFEATED
MAYA · ANGELOU

NEVERTHELESS
SHE
PERSISTED.
McDONNELL

Don't let circumstances define you. Push the boundaries and always be true to yourself.

Oprah Winfrey became the first African American female to host a nationally syndicated daily talk show in 1986. She is a dedicated activist for children's rights, a staunch advocate for female education, and supports various charitable projects that help improve the quality of life for women around the world.

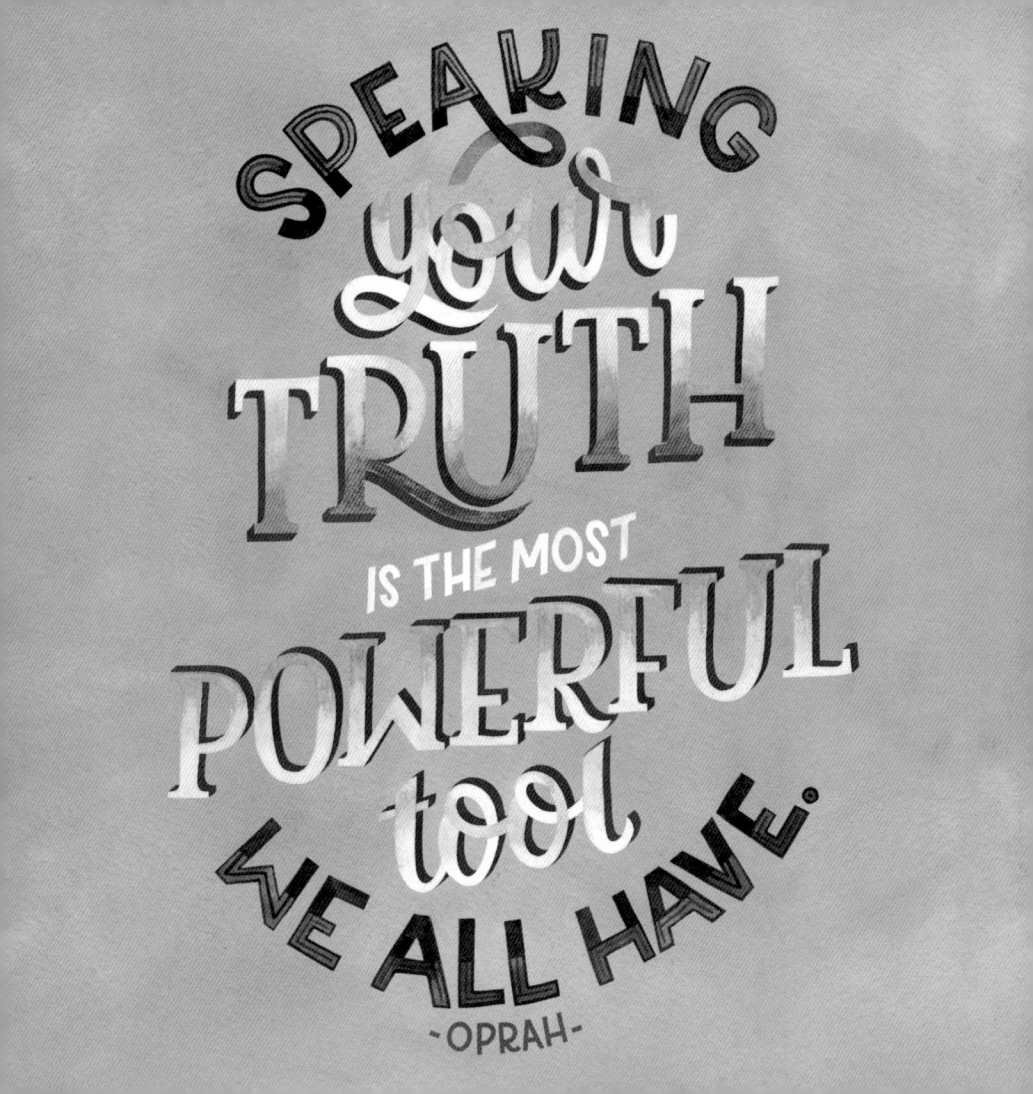
SPEAKING
your
TRUTH
IS THE MOST
POWERFUL
tool
WE ALL HAVE.
-OPRAH-

She believed
SHE COULD,
so
SHE DID.
R.S. Grey, Scoring Wilder

confidence:

noun • CON·FI·DENCE \kanfədəns/

a feeling of self-assurance arising from one's appreciation of one's own abilities or qualities

Never settle.

Never give up.

Never stop believing in yourself.

YOU are WORTH it.

I LOVE
the
person
I'VE BECOME
because
I FOUGHT TO
become HER
Kaci
Diane

YOU MUST NEVER be FEARFUL about what you are DOING WHEN IT is RIGHT.
ROSA PARKS

ROSA PARKS, an African American woman whose refusal to give up her seat on a bus to a white man, ignited the U.S. Civil Rights movement in 1955. She believed that differences of race, nationality, or religion should not be used to deny any human being citizenship rights or privileges.

Determination:

noun • DE·TER·MI·NA·TION /de,terme'naSH(ə)n/

firmness of purpose, resoluteness

Empowered
WOMEN
EMPOWER
women

THEY TRIED TO
bury
us
THEY DIDN'T KNOW
we were
SEEDS
MEXICAN PROVERB

Step outside your
comfort zone and accept
life's challenges.
Only then will you grow.

At an early age, COCO CHANEL experienced poverty, the death of her mother, and the abandonment of her father. Using her resourcefulness, she launched a global fashion empire that dominated the haute couture scene for decades.

BEAUTY
BEGINS the MOMENT
YOU DECIDE
to be
YOURSELF
Coco Chanel

YOU
are
ALWAYS
ENOUGH

SELF•LOVE:

noun • SELF·LOVE \self'lav/

regard for one's own well-being and happiness

TODAY
is the day
that will
change your life.

START where you are.
USE WHAT YOU HAVE.
DO what you can.

IF you WANT THE
RAINBOW
you
GOTTA
PUT UP WITH
the
rain
DOLLY PARTON

Prompted by her father's inability to read, Grammy Award-winning country singer DOLLY PARTON created a book-gifting program to fight illiteracy. IMAGINATION LIBRARY is a world-wide charity that provides free books to young children.

PASSION:

noun • PAS·SION /paSHeN/
strong and barely
controllable emotion

Have
NO FEAR
YOU WILL FIND your way
IT'S IN your bones
IT'S IN YOUR SOUL
MARK Z DANIELEWSKI

i figure if a
GIRL
WANTS TO BE A
LEGEND,
SHE SHOULD JUST
go ahead
&
BE ONE.
-CALAMITY JANE-

Be the person who

INSPIRES

OTHERS

PERSIST

BECCA·CAHAN